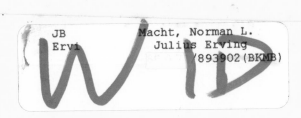

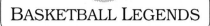

BASKETBALL LEGENDS

Kareem Abdul-Jabbar

Larry Bird

Wilt Chamberlain

Julius Erving

Magic Johnson

Michael Jordan

CHELSEA HOUSE PUBLISHERS

BASKETBALL LEGENDS

JULIUS ERVING

Norman L. Macht

Introduction by
Chuck Daly

CHELSEA HOUSE PUBLISHERS
New York · Philadelphia

Produced by Daniel Bial Agency
New York, New York.

Picture research by Alan Gottlieb
Cover illustration by Richard Leonard

3 5 7 9 8 6 4 2

Macht, Norman L.
    Julius Erving / Norman L. Macht.
      p.   cm. — (Basketball legends)
    Includes bibliographical references and index.
    ISBN 0-7910-2429-6 (hard) $14.95
    1. Erving, Julius—Juvenile literature. 2. Basketball players—
United States—Biography—Juvenile literature. [1. Erving, Julius.
2. Basketball players. 3. Afro-Americans—Biography.]
    I. Title. II. Series.
    GV884.I79M33 1994
    796.323'092—dc20
    [B]   94-5777
                                                              CIP
                                                              AC

CONTENTS

Becoming a
Basketball Legend

Chuck Daly

What does it take to be a basketball superstar? Two of the three things it takes are easy to spot. Any great athlete must have excellent skills and tremendous dedication. The third quality needed is much harder to define, or even put in words. Others call it leadership or desire to win, but I'm not sure that explains it fully. This third quality relates to the athlete's thinking process, a certain mentality and work ethic. One can coach athletic skills, and while few superstars need outside influence to help keep them dedicated, it is possible for a coach to offer some well-timed words in order to keep that athlete fully motivated. But a coach can do no more than appeal to a player's will to win; how much that player is then capable of ensuring victory is up to his own internal workings.

In recent times, we have been fortunate to have seen some of the best to play the game. Larry Bird, Magic Johnson, and Michael Jordan had all three components of superstardom in full measure. They brought their teams to numerous championships, and made the players around them better. (They also made their coaches look smart.)

I myself coached a player who belongs in that class, Isiah Thomas, who helped lead the Detroit Pistons to consecutive NBA crowns. Isiah is not tall—he's just over six feet—but he could do whatever he wanted with the ball. And what he wanted to do most was lead and win.

All the players I mentioned above and those whom this

series will chronicle are tremendously gifted athletes, but for the most part, you can't play professional basketball at all unless you have excellent skills. And few players get to stay on their team unless they are willing to dedicate themselves to improving their talents even more, learning about their opponents, and finding a way to join with their teammates and win.

It's that third element that separates the good player from the superstar, the memorable players from the legends of the game. Superstars know when to take over the game. If the situation calls for a defensive stop, the superstars stand up and do it. If the situation calls for a key pass, they make it. And if the situation calls for a big shot, they want the ball. They don't want the ball simply because of their own glory or ego. Instead they know—and their teammates know—that they are the ones who can deliver, regardless of the pressure.

The words "legend" and "superstar" are often tossed around without real meaning. Taking a hard look at some of those who truly can be classified as "legends" can provide insight into the things that brought them to that level. All of them developed their legacy over numerous seasons of play, even if certain games will always stand out in the memories of those who saw them. Those games typically featured amazing feats of all-around play. No matter how great the fans thought the superstars, the players were capable yet of surprising them, their opponents, and occasionally even themselves. The desire to win took over, and with their dedication and athletic skills already in place, they were capable of the most astonishing achievements.

CHUCK DALY, most recently the head coach of the New Jersey Nets, guided the Detroit Pistons to two straight NBA championships, in 1989 and 1990. He earned a gold medal as coach of the 1992 U.S. Olympic basketball team—the so-called "Dream Team"—and was inducted into the Pro Basketball Hall of Fame in 1994.

SLAM DUNK

On May 10, 1976, the American Basketball Association (ABA) came up with a new gimmick to add to their All-Star Game. They held a slam-dunk contest.

The ABA was 10 years old, but they were still struggling to stay in business and compete with the more established National Basketball Association (NBA). They had tried numerous gimmicks before: adding the three-point shot, using a red, white, and blue ball, and displaying sexy cheerleaders. They also featured flashy players who were willing to put on a show (as opposed to the more staid type of play typically found in the NBA). Still, people thought that their talent level was inferior to that of the NBA. The ABA was viewed as basketball's flying circus, filled with slammers, alley oopers, fancy dribblers, and few team players.

Nothing more clearly showed the difference between the two leagues than the addition of the

Dr. J was the original high flyer. Here he soars over Fly Williams in a game against the St. Louis Spirits.

slam-dunk contest. The slam dunk is the epitome of the playground game, featuring spectacular, improvised moves. A dunk artist is like a jazz musician, improvising at top speed, daring the next player to "top this." One could easily imagine the owners of NBA teams shuddering, thinking how desperate the ABA must be to stage such a low form of basketball.

The five entries in the contest represented the ABA at its colorful best. Only Larry Kenon of the group did not have a catchy nickname; the other four were George Gervin ("The Ice Man"), David Thompson ("Skywalker"), Artis Gilmore ("A-Train"), and Julius Erving ("Dr. J"). Each was to perform five dunks. In anticipation of the explosions the players might wreak, the ABA had two extra backboards and rims on hand.

Gilmore, Kenon, and Gervin each missed an early dunk. The capacity crowd of 15,021 in Denver's McNichols Arena stood and cheered the home town Nuggets' David Thompson. Though only 6'4", Thompson had been described as "8'4" off the backboard" when he led North Carolina State University to the 1974 NCAA championship. He was Erving's greatest ABA rival when it came to floating through the air, dunking, rebounding, stealing, and shot blocking.

Julius Erving took the competition seriously. He saw it as "an opportunity in a team sport for an individual to express himself in a memorable way. If you fly or hang in the air so long in a way that only you can do, it's a great rush." Before the game, he had practiced his moves without a ball for 15 minutes in the lockerroom.

In the five years since he had shown up at a Virginia Squires rookie camp, Erving had been making plays that nobody had ever seen before.

He flew higher, floated longer, and bounded farther in a single leap than veteran coaches and players believed possible. At 6'6" and 200 pounds, he was a tad shorter and smaller than the average forward. But whatever he gave away in inches and pounds he made up for with speed, touch, leaping ability, thinking ability, and sheer trickery. When Dr. J was not playing, he was devising, imagining, and even dreaming of new moves in his sleep.

Meanwhile, opposing coaches devised, imagined, and were reduced to dreaming of effective means of stopping him. Although Erving's flashy actions earned him the tag of "hot dog," everything he did was geared toward winning. He had learned to gauge the tempo and balance of a game for a quarter before deciding when and how best to improvise a hot lick here and there for its greatest impact on the outcome of the game.

One coach lamented, "My whole defense against him is to stop him from going into his high-wire act. When he does that, his team gets excited and your players want to stop and applaud, too."

Kentucky Colonels coach Hubie Brown ordered his players to foul Dr. J if he was coming toward them on a fast break. "I didn't care if he was 20 feet from the basket. Just foul him be-

Following the 1976 slam-dunk contest, Julius Erving led the way in the All-Star Game. Here he scores two points surrounded by (left to right) Bobby Jones, Dan Issel, Billy Thompson (number 25), and David Thompson.

fore he took off. If you didn't foul him and he dunked, it was a $50 fine."

David Thompson finished his fifth slam—a leaping, spinning pirouette that ended with the ball jammed hard through the hoop. The crowd went wild.

Erving ignored the ovation. That was an old trick. He had done it himself a few years earlier after an ABA publicist had told him that only two players, Darrell Griffith and Thompson, could turn a 360-degree dunk. A few seconds later Dr. J walked off the court and said, "Make that three."

After making two compulsory routine jams, Dr. J chose what he called his Iron Cross. He leaped from the left side past the basket and jammed the ball through the hoop behind his head without looking.

For his next riff, he charged the basket head on, and soared almost beyond it, grabbing the rim with his left hand and thrusting the ball through the net to the floor below like a clap of thunder. It reminded his New York Nets coach, Kevin Loughery, of the first game he had ever coached the Doctor.

"Doc drove the baseline and found himself under the basket with two big guys going for the block. Somehow, Doc floated between them and then almost tore the rim down with a slam. That was the greatest dunk I had ever seen."

The excited chatter of the crowd shut down when Erving picked up two brightly colored balls and stood calmly with his back to the basket. Suddenly, he lifted off, twisted, and jammed one, then the other, like the arms of a runaway windmill. When his size 15 sneakers hit ground again, the crowd shook the seats with a roar.

Julius Erving could have rolled in a gentle layup on his last effort and still been crowned the most spectacular of them all. But that was not his style. With Thompson soundly beaten, it was time to challenge his own limitations.

Nobody had ever seen a dunk from the free-throw line, 15 feet out. Standing at the far end of the court, Dr. J envisioned himself doing it. The picture came into clearer focus as he began dribbling down the court. The crowd was hushed. Every eye followed him as he raced to the free-throw line and took off, soaring unbelievably high and long, soaring, soaring straight for the circle of iron, and delivering the gaudy ball perfectly through the net.

Some called it flashy. Some called it showmanship. But it was also a beautiful sight to behold. Even today, when the name of Julius Erving is mentioned, the first thing many people recall is that moment when Dr. J soared with balletic grace and raised the art of basketball to a never-before-imagined level.

Erving's capture of the ABA's slam-dunk contest helped change the history of the NBA. As Dr. J and Skywalker Thompson and others brought the playground style of play to the world of professional basketball, the moguls of the NBA realized that they could ignore its popularity no longer. The key to their own future prosperity was right under their noses.

Not all were ready to admit it. "Julius Erving is a nice kid," sniffed Red Auerbach, coach of the NBA's mighty Boston Celtics. "But he's not a great player."

Every kid on every blacktop playground court knew better.

2

I WANT TO BE A DOCTOR

Julius Winfield Erving, Jr., was born on February 22, 1950, in Hempstead, New York, a town on Long Island about 25 miles east of New York City. His mother, Callie Mae Erving, called him June, short for Junior.

A few years later, Julius Erving, Sr., left his three children—Alexis, June, and Marvin—in the care of Callie Mae. Julius had little chance to know his father, who was hit and killed by a car when June was 11.

The daughter of sharecroppers in South Carolina, Callie Mae Erving worked days as a cleaning woman. The family received some social help, but there was always food on the table. Still, "when I asked her for sneakers that were better, she got them," Julius recalled. "We didn't ask her for much, but if we wanted it, she got it."

Mrs. Erving trusted God to keep her kids out of trouble during the day while she was working. But in the evenings she added a dose of disci-

Julius Erving holds the trophy from an early champion team.

pline to her faith, teaching the three youngsters right from wrong and backing up the lessons with a firm hand.

"I learned early that when I made a wrong decision I was punished," Julius said. "Conversely, doing the right thing always brought rewards."

June was the quiet one. His sister was talkative, and little Marvin kept things lively, but June preferred to watch and listen and learn. "I consciously tried to be aware of what was happening around me," he said. He learned from his mother's example of self-reliance and sense of responsibility in dealing with life's challenges.

Although there was no official segregation where the Ervings lived, most of the black families dwelt in the "colored section" of town and the elementary schools they attended were mostly black. But the junior high and high schools were integrated. The Supreme Court's 1954 decision banning segregated schools touched off fierce battles to prevent the changes in the South. Newspapers and television news were filled with reports of National Guard troops escorting black kids into previously all-white schools through crowds of hostile whites. Civil rights demonstrations occurred in many states, as blacks demanded equal job opportunities, equal education, and the right to shop in the same stores, eat at the same restaurants, and use the same public restrooms as their white fellow citizens. Pride became a paramount watchword for blacks.

The drive for pride extended even to the playgrounds, where competition to outdo the other kids dominated every activity. Julius had his first taste of it when he was six years old. Kids playing on the swings in the nearby park played a game called Geronimo. (American paratroopers in World War II used to shout "Geronimo" as they leaped out of airplanes to the battlefields below.)

In the game, Julius would pump and swing as high as he could, then, at the peak of his upward arc, spring off the swing, yelling, "Geronimo." He flew through the air, trying to see how far away he could land, or how long he could stay in the air, or perhaps try to perform a somersault before landing. If he made a good jump and not crashed in a heap, he would look back at the next kid and dare him to "match that."

Julius loved the feeling of soaring through the air and quickly discovered that he was the best Geronimo player in the Linder Avenue housing project. In one leap, he could move his head and shoulders one way and his legs another, wiggle toward a landing in one spot, and come down in another.

The Erving children also took pride in their schoolwork. Their mother impressed on them the importance of an education as a means of achieving a better life, "to make each day better than the one before and to improve each task, however small." Julius was not shy in the classroom and was proud to have won a poetry recitation contest.

Looking for some physical activity more challenging than Geronimo, June came upon the crude blacktop basketball courts at nearby Campbell Park. He watched fascinated as older boys dodged, spun, reversed direction, and cut through a crowd of opponents, all while maintaining a steady thump-thump-thump rhythm with the bouncing ball. He marveled as they

In high school, Julius Erving dreamed more about basketball as a ticket to a college education than as a ticket to a pro career.

suddenly leaped high above outstretched arms and gracefully arced the ball through the metal ring. He tried to absorb everything he saw, his body copying the shifts and turns as he studied the feints and fakes employed by shooters as they drove toward the basket. His eyes grew wide when a ball handler, surrounded by three or four bodies, miraculously emerged high above the crowd and slammed the ball through the net to the pavement below.

"I loved to watch what guys would do in emergency situations," he recalled.

Julius Erving was hooked. From then on, every free minute from school and homework found him on the blacktop court. At nine years old, he was small and skinny, but he had long arms and unusually large hands. Already he could palm the 30-inch round ball with no trouble.

For hours on end, as often as not alone, he experimented, practicing his shooting, trying out moves and fakes and leaps and slams. In one-on-one games or pickup games, he found an outlet for his intelligence and creativity, as well as a release from the pent-up emotions he had been unable to articulate with words.

"When there was a fight at home or I was uptight, I would go down to the park and play," he said, "sometimes just by myself. And when I was through, I would be feeling good again. I could come back and deal with the situation."

His mother noticed the change, the new-found intensity and focus of interest. "I really didn't see June doing anything steadily until he took up playing ball," she recalled.

Julius had no father, no coaches, no older brothers to teach him. When he was not on the court, he choreographed moves and patterns in his head, until he could take them to the court. The absence of any guidance may have resulted in wasted motion and energy, but it also freed his imagination from all restraints. There was nobody to say "don't" or "you can't do this."

"I set no dimensions for my game," he said. "I always went to the basket."

June's first exposure to formal coaching came when he joined a local Salvation Army team for ages 10 to 12. But by then he had taken his own approach to the game far beyond the fundamentals preached by the coach, Don Ryan. Led by the aggressive, acrobatic 5'6" Julius, the team won 27 and lost 3 against similar teams in the area. The next year, they won 31 out of 32.

The bus rides to other towns and the hospitality of people connected with the host teams gave Julius his first glimpse of "how people lived on the other side of the fence. Big houses, two cars, color TV. I wondered what you had to do to get them."

But he already had an idea of the course he could take to get them. One day in school, his teacher asked him to tell the class what he wanted to be when he grew up. Without hesitating, he replied, "I want to be a doctor."

When Julius was 14, his mother remarried and the family moved a few miles away to the town of Roosevelt. Julius immediately set out to establish himself as King of the Courts at Roosevelt Park, a mile from his home. As the new kid in town, he had to prove himself against the reigning hot shots, many of whom were older and bigger. Relying on his quickness and imagination, Julius dazzled them with moves and

Ray Wilson coached Dr. J in high school and later coached at the University of Massachusetts.

dunks the likes of which they had never seen. Roosevelt High's freshman basketball coach, Earl Moseley, was among the spectators. "It wasn't long before Jewel owned that park," he said.

Julius avidly watched the few college and pro games that were broadcast on television. "My palms would sweat, and I'd think of moves no one else had done. I'd learn by watching good guys and bad guys. I'd dream up fantastic moves and then go out on the court and make them work."

Sometimes it took weeks of practice to make them work, in hours of solitary practice or in one-on-one games to 100 points.

The quest for pride drove the competitors on the green asphalt court just as it had done in the Geronimo games on the playground swings. The outcome of a pickup game was measured not merely by who scored the most points, but also by how badly you beat the guy defending you.

"There's a whole psychology in the playground game," Julius explained, "that makes you want to beat a guy in a way that makes him pay twice. You want to outscore him and you also want to freak him out with a big move or a big block. That way even if the score is tied, you and he both know you're really ahead."

Often the players who came out second best on the court tried to salvage some pride with their fists. But Moseley said he never remembered seeing Jewel in a fight or an argument. "He was never a street hanger. He would never hang out drinking wine like so many other kids did. If you wanted Julius, you always knew where to find him—in the park or at school."

Julius let his moves and airborne acrobatics speak for him; he saw no need to brag or talk trash to his opponents. He knew he was good, but he believed there had to have been thousands of other kids on other playgrounds who could do the same things he did. Even when he traveled to other parks on Long Island—outflying, outrebounding, outslamming everybody—Julius still considered basketball as just a game, a source of fun and pride, nothing more. One of the opponents he gave a lesson to was a tall kid named Lew Alcindor who had already drawn a lot of attention. Alcindor would later become even more famous under the name Kareem Abdul-Jabbar.

Despite his successes, Julius kept a calm head. Education remained his first priority. He even considered his social life more important than hoops.

By the fall of 1966, the 16-year-old junior had grown to 6'3", although his bushy Afro made him seem taller. He was easily the best player on the varsity, but the coach, Ray Wilson, had five talented seniors who had played together since junior high, and they were determined to form the starting five in their final year.

Although playground basketball required a strong ego to compete with all the other strong egos, Julius was able to accept the role of bench player. Armed with the self-confidence and security rooted in a strong family, he never complained about lack of playing time or not getting to start the games. He was a team player whose sole goal was to win.

Despite seldom seeing action until the second quarter of a game, Julius led the team in scoring and rebounds. His appearance on the floor triggered a perceptible shift in the rhythm and pace of a game. His attacks on the basket inspired one sportswriter to describe him as "a young boy with the body control of an accomplished ballet dancer."

In his senior year, Julius was the undisputed star of the team, but he never acted like a star. Once, after missing a bus to a practice scrimmage, he took a one-game suspension without protest and without explaining that he and his friends had stopped to help a teacher whose car was stuck in the snow.

Aided by two outstanding players who had transferred from New York City schools, Erving again led the team in scoring and rebounds en route to a 16-1 record. Although college scouts were in the crowd at every game, they focused more on the outside shooters from the city. Julius paid them less attention than they gave him; his sights were set no further than winning the Nassau County championship. Roosevelt High won the playoff opener, 82-48; Julius had 28 points and 11 rebounds. But their next opponent, Elmont High, slowed the pace and applied too much muscle. Roosevelt lost, 62-49.

Following his graduation in the spring of 1968, Julius visited a basketball camp in upstate New York. He was invited to square off in a one-on-one match against Wayne Embry, a center on the world champion Boston Celtics. The NBA veteran was four inches taller and 70 pounds heavier than the soft-spoken Julius.

"I was going to muscle this skinny kid," Embry said, "but I couldn't catch him. He drove around me, he dunked over me. I was an NBA center and I had lost to a high school kid."

Despite running rings around other NBA stars at the camp, Julius still considered basketball as nothing more than a ticket to a college education. He visited campuses in the Midwest and New England, but did not draw much interest. Besides, he did not want to go far from home anyhow; his brother Marvin's health, never strong, seemed to be weakening. His sister too would soon marry and move away.

With the help of Coach Wilson, Julius chose the University of Massachusetts, in the small town of Amherst, about 200 miles from home. Wilson was a friend of Jack Leaman, the UMass coach, and he believed Julius would be more comfortable in the small-town atmosphere.

In the 1960s, UMass had a strong basketball program, often going to postseason tournaments. But two college athletic rules in effect at the time influenced Erving's career. Freshmen were not allowed to play varsity sports, and the slam dunk was not allowed in the college game. The playground game developed on urban asphalt courts was unknown in the rest of the country, where the long-distance set shot still predominated. This

Coach Jack Leaman said, "We made Julius play team offense and team defense, We set it up so that he could handle a lot of situations he would face in the pros, situations that many college hotshots had trouble handling."

rule forced Erving to develop and improve the other aspects of his game, making him a more versatile and complete player. He could dribble the ball the length of the court at top speed, stop and hit an outside jump shot with alarming precision, or make a crisp pass to a teammate cutting toward the basket.

UMass' varsity team had a very successful year, racking up an 18-6 record. But the freshman team was the talk of the campus thanks to their 16-0 record and Julius's flamboyant performances in taking the ball to the hoop.

It began to occur to Erving that maybe he was doing things that most other players could not do. "It was a shock," he said, "but when a hundred people tell you you're different, then a thousand people tell you you're different, you just say to yourself, 'Okay, I'm different.'"

On February 22, his mother and brother came up to Amherst, Massachusetts, to see the freshmen play. At halftime, the entire crowd sang happy birthday to Julius. When he went home for spring break a few weeks later, Marvin was in the hospital suffering from a fatal form of lupus. Julius was unaware of the seriousness of Marvin's condition; his brother had always been sickly. But soon after he returned to school, Julius had to return home to help bury his brother.

"I cried all day on the day of the funeral," he recalled. "I went to the cemetery the first few days after he was buried and I cried each day. I told myself I wasn't going to cry anymore, ever. I was really brought to my knees and made to feel helpless and powerless. It was like I had no control. I could be gone tomorrow."

That summer, Julius lived at home and worked at the same playground in Hempstead where he had been introduced to basketball. In the late afternoons, after the games had ended and the kids gone home, he dribbled and shot and thought and solemnly practiced some new moves. He pondered about life, and how people fit into the world.

"I felt helpless," he said, "but I also became fearless. I felt, 'Well, if I'm going to do something, I'm going to let it all hang out.'"

3

THE DOCTOR GOES TO SCHOOL

In 1970, with scant television coverage of college basketball, it was possible for Julius Erving to lead the Massachusetts Minutemen to an 18-7 record and a berth in the prestigious National Invitations Tournament (NIT) in New York City's Madison Square Garden, average more than 20 points and almost 20 rebounds a game (which was second in the nation), and still be unknown to most basketball fans. But by the end of that summer, the legend of Dr. J was born.

The Rucker League in Harlem was the big league of summer playground basketball. The fenced-in asphalt court on 155th Street in New York City was surrounded by bleachers that would be filled with aficionados of the game who came to watch future Hall of Famers such as Wilt Chamberlain, Willis Reed, and Kareem

Julius Erving was the greatest basketball player in Yankee Conference history. He led the University of Massachusetts to postseason play in 1970 and 1971. Here he goes in for two points against St. Anselm.

Abdul-Jabbar develop their skills. Kids climbed trees and watched from rooftops. They did not care who won or lost. They came, as circus fans who gaze agape at acrobats on the high wire, to see young men fake out and float in midair and finger roll. They came to thrill to the power of a vicious slam dunk, or the block of another's shot high off the backboard. The young men who played brought treasured reputations and enduring nicknames: Jumping Jackie, who could reject a shot two and a half feet above the rim; the Helicopter; the Goat.

Julius, an unknown kid from Long Island, tore defenses to shreds with his moves. He quickly became the favorite of the cheering, foot-stomping spectators. In one game, he scored 53 points. One slam was memorable: He charged toward the basket, all five defenders converging on him. Julius planted his feet and leaped high into the air; as he sailed past the backboard, he reached out and grabbed the rim with his left hand. Then he slammed the ball through the hoop with his huge right. The ball hit the pavement with such force that it bounced back up through the chain metal net and came down through it again. The explosion of screaming fans shook the neighborhood.

Some viewers swore they once saw him pass to himself. Trapped by three defenders on the sideline, Julius flung the ball high off the backboard, ran to the other side of the court, leaped high for the rebound, and slammed it home.

Ever since high school, Julius and a buddy had called each other by nicknames. Julius tagged his friend, "The Professor," and the friend called Julius, "The Doctor." But it had remained a private joke between them.

All summer the Rucker public address announcer groped for an appropriately descriptive nickname for the new phenom. He tried Little Hawk, Black Moses, Houdini, Magic, and The Claw. Finally, with some annoyance, Julius went over to the name-coiner. "Listen," he said. "I already have a nickname: The Doctor." And so he would be known for the rest of his life.

When he was not playing in the Rucker League, Julius visited Long Island courts where pro stars practiced. He more than held his own against them. Invited to the U.S. Olympic camp in Colorado, he discovered that he was as good as the highly publicized All-Americans from the Big Ten and Pacific Coast conferences. Even though he was younger than most others and not from a powerhouse university that had a tradition of turning out NBA material, Julius led the team in scoring and rebounds. He did not make the Olympic team, but he began to think there might be a future for him in the game.

Back on the college court in his junior year, the Doctor was forced to put many of his colorful moves in storage. Coach Leaman favored a deliberate ball-control style over the fast break. While this held down Julius's scoring, he still averaged 26.9 points and 19.5 rebounds in Yankee Conference play. And it enabled him to improve his passing and defense.

Many UMass fans preferred to watch Dr. J practice, where he could let out all the stops, rather than see him play a conference game. "The fieldhouse was standing room only during practice sessions," recalled Mike Flanagan, a freshman who scrimmaged against the varsity. "I was a country kid from New Hampshire, where long set shots were our game. In one scrimmage

I came down the court and pulled up at the top of the key to take an 18-footer. I was wide open. Julius was at least 10 feet away from me. No threat, I thought. But he came out of nowhere and blocked it before I could get it away. I realized right then that I better develop a slider and concentrate on baseball," said the future 20-game winner for the Baltimore Orioles.

The Doctor was not completely subdued in conference games. Without the aid of instant replay, he could make reporters hesitate to write what they saw, as when he started a play in one corner and with one bound completed a layup on the other side of the lane.

Following a 23-3 season—the best in school history—the Minutemen were invited back to the NIT, where they lost to the University of North Carolina in the first round. Playing before many pro scouts in the packed Garden, Julius was out of step all night, got into foul trouble early, and suffered his worst game of the year.

Following his disappointing performance in the NIT loss, the Doctor was giving no thought to professional basketball as he packed his gear and looked ahead to his senior year at UMass. Unknown to him, the general manager of the Virginia Squires of the ABA was sitting in Norfolk, Virginia, studying fuzzy black and white films of Julius in action. He liked what he saw and inquired if the Doctor was interested. Disdaining the NBA's rule preventing the signing of college players until their classes graduated, the ABA went after anyone they thought would fit their flamboyant style and draw customers. The Doctor was a natural.

Julius said no. But he was curious to know how much the pros thought he was worth. He

was stunned when he found out: $500,000 for a four-year contract.

"The offer made me start thinking about how many hours I had spent playing ball," he said. "I then realized, in all honesty, my main preference was playing basketball. It was a chance to change my financial situation for life."

Like a prisoner strapped into leg irons, Julius looked forward to being freed to play his game. "I hadn't been allowed to dunk in competition for four years," he said. Now the chains would be off. He would be free to fly and slam and try out all the moves he had envisioned.

"Sometimes when I start a play," he had said, "I never know if I will be able to do what I would like. But I always go ahead and try. I guess it's sort of like daring to be great."

The University of North Carolina bounced UMass from the 1971 NIT finals in the first round. Denny Wuycik scored this layup as the Doctor could do little but watch.

4

CHANGING THE GAME

Julius Erving created the kind of basketball that became the ABA game. Before he arrived on the pro scene, the game followed a predictable script: the big men stayed close to the basket, rebounding, blocking shots, and scoring on hooks and layups. The smaller, faster men handled the ball and shot primarily from the outside.

As a small forward, the Doctor combined the two roles in one, breaking open the pattern and creating more scoring opportunities for his teammates and more excitement for the fans. Freed of the restraints of the college game, Julius wanted to do everything, be everywhere— rebound, block shots, charge the hoop, shoot from the outside, and, above all, dunk, dunk, dunk.

"I loved every minute of it," he said of his early ABA years. "Basketball was truly a game.

Dr. J led the Virginia Squires to the ABA playoffs in 1972, his rookie year, but they lost to his future team, the New York Nets.

Dr. J averaged an eye-popping 28.7 points per game during his five years in the ABA. He scored his 10,000th point in this game against the St. Louis Spirits.

There were few hassles, and on the court we were freewheeling."

When he showed up at the Squires' rookie camp in Norfolk in the summer of 1971, the first thing his new coach, Al Bianchi, noticed was his huge hands. "My God, did you see those meat hooks?" he exclaimed.

Other players were initially awed by Doc's billowing six-inch Afro, the biggest they had ever seen. But it did not take long for all eyes to be riveted on the rookie's moves. Free to try whatever his fertile imagination could invent, he amazed teammates and opponents alike in every game by introducing three or four moves they had never seen before. Coaches became concerned that their players were too distracted to defend against him effectively.

Not everyone was happy to see Erving capturing the spotlight. Envious of the rookie's popularity, teammate Charlie Scott hogged the ball and put up 30 shots a game in an effort to win the league scoring title to draw some attention to himself. The rest of the team knew what was happening. "I knew it," Bianchi said. "He knew it. Julie knew it. Julie was mature enough to accept it and to fit his game to the fact."

Erving used his rebounding skills on the offensive board to average 27 points a game. Scott jumped to the NBA before the season ended, and Erving led all players in the playoffs in scoring, rebounds, and assists. But the Squires lost in the semifinals to the New York Nets, four games to two.

The 7'2" Artis Gilmore won the Rookie of the Year Award, but Erving was already being compared to future Hall of Famer Elgin Baylor, whose career in the NBA ended that year. In fact, Coach Bianchi claimed, "Julie could rebound better, run better, played defense a heck of a lot better, and shoot with both hands."

Coaches, fans, and writers called Erving "Jewel," "Julie," and "Doc," but after his roommate, Willie Sojourner, refined it to "Dr. J," the other appellations were seldom heard.

The praise did not go unnoticed by Dr. J. It did not turn his head or change his quiet, thoughtful personality. But it made him think that if people thought he was as good as the top stars in either league he should be paid accordingly.

The Squires said they could not afford to give him a raise. And Erving believed they did not intend to honor the deferred payments part of the contract. Meanwhile, NBA teams were waving big contracts at top ABA stars to lure them away and weaken the rival league. So Erving hired an agent in April 1972. The agent quickly negotiated a five-year contract with the Atlanta Hawks that included a $250,000 bonus, an apartment in Atlanta, and a new blue Jaguar. But the Squires were still in the playoffs, so the deal was kept quiet. The NBA held its draft on April 10, and the Milwaukee Bucks selected Erving despite rumors of the Atlanta deal.

Erving spent that summer in Atlanta, traveling north for some action in the Rucker League. But most of the action was taking place in another court—the law court—where the Bucks, Hawks, and Squires fought for possession of Dr. J. In September, he began playing exhibition games with the Hawks, despite the NBA's decision than he belonged to the Bucks. In October, when the court ruled that Erving could only play for the Squires until an arbitrator could sort it all out, Dr. J took the decision in stride and returned to Norfolk for the 1972-73 season.

Unaffected by the legal sideshow, he led the league in scoring with an average of 31.9 points per game. He also rated sixth in rebounds and third in steals. He matured as a team player, cutting back on his airborne dunks and limiting his nightly introduction of eye-popping new moves to one or two strategically timed inventions. But when he did improvise, they were beauts. One night, against San Diego, he snatched an offensive rebound and leaped high in the air to pass off to an open man. Just then a defender came between them. Still at the peak of his leap, as he realized the pass would be intercepted, he spied another open Squire, spun around in a full circle, switched the ball to his left hand, and pushed it to the open man, who put up an easy layup before Dr. J returned to earth.

Players on both benches shook their heads and looked at each other. After the game, a San Diego coach ran over to Erving. "Man, I thought I'd seen everything," he said. "But that 360 degree job, nobody's ever done anything like that. It was unbelievable."

The legal squabble over what uniform Dr. J would wear was resolved when the New York Nets of the ABA bought out his contract from the Squires following the 1972-73 season for $750,000. They also paid $500,000 to settle the Hawks' claim and made Dr. J happy with an eight-year $2.8 million contract.

New York was home grounds for the Doctor, and the Big Apple provided the biggest spotlight in pro sports. The Nets were hungry for a championship and they expected the Doctor to deliver it for them. At the press conference to announce his signing, reporters asked Erving if the pressure of playing in New York would affect him.

"I put the most pressure on myself because of my ambitions to be the best basketball player ever," the 23-year-old New York native replied. "What happens around me can't put any more pressure on me than that." Then Dr. J. got into his white Avanti with his initials on the license plates and drove out of the city, past the Nassau Coliseum where he would be appearing for the Nets, to the park in Roosevelt where he had practiced for hours as a kid.

Julius Erving with his children Cheo (left) and Julius.

Bobby Jones of the Denver Nuggets tries to block Dr. J's shot in the 1976 ABA playoffs as Dan Issel hopes for a rebound.

"My lifestyle has changed considerably," he told a reporter as he swapped high-fives with the players on the green asphalt courts. "But I still want to identify with my roots. There are certain things you can't buy in life. I'm very much aware of that. There are things here I don't want to give up. Things like friendships and memories of people who have affected my growth and development."

After winning four of their first five games, the Nets fell into last place on a 10-game losing streak early in the 1972-73 season. The reason for the swoon was clear to the coaches, who took the blame. Awed by Dr. J's defensive prowess in practice, when his long arms and huge hands disrupted all who tried to dribble or pass by him, head coach Kevin Loughery had decided to use a full court press for the entire 48 minutes of every game. It soon became apparent that nobody could maintain that pace game after game. Admitting his mistake, the coach abandoned the strategy and the Nets took off, winning 19 of their next 22.

Dr. J became the team leader, not only in scoring, but by giving a man who missed a pass an encouraging word, boosting a rookie's confidence, accentuating the positive with constructive criticism, and blending with the individual talents of the other players to produce a winning ensemble.

The 6'10" rookie Larry Kenon complemented Erving at the other forward position. When defenses keyed on Dr J., Mr. K stuck the short jumpers and blasted the slams. At center, 6'11" Billy Paultz, a mound of flesh called "The Whopper," was a formidable fixture under the basket. In the backcourt, Brian Taylor was the ballhandler and Super John Williamson the punishing physical presence. Late in the season the Nets added a ball-hawking guard, Mike Gale, and a hustling "enforcer," Wendell Ladner, to their bench.

Unlike some stars, Erving left behind the one-on-one playground mindset when it came time to play as a team. "I honestly feel there are guys in the pros who have never stopped thinking that way," he said, "and it restricts their usefulness. They may end up as high scorers, but they haven't helped their teams."

He remained cool at all times, never got into fights or swapped trash talk on the court. If a situation arose that called for an apology, he was the first to offer it, even if he did not feel responsible.

During one game, after Dr. J had put on a sustained display of whirling, swarming, floating, and dunking, Coach Loughery suddenly called a time out. When the puzzled players gathered on the sidelines, Loughery looked straight at Erving and said, "I called that time out because I wanted to tell you that you've just played the greatest three-minutes stretch of basketball I have ever seen."

Until Erving's arrival in New York, the Knicks had dominated the basketball headlines and conversation in the city. Now, Dr. J was crowding the 1973 NBA champs out of the picture. One week he appeared on the cover of both *Sports Illustrated* and *The Sporting News*. The Doctor in New York and Wilt Chamberlain coaching in San Diego gave the ABA a quantum leap in respectability and exposure.

On February 9, with the Nets comfortably atop the Eastern Division, Dr. J was married. Preferring to keep his private life just that—private—he was upset when word got out about the name of the New York hotel where the wedding would take place. Invited guests, fans, re-

Roy Boe hugged Erving in the lockerroom after Dr. J scored 31 points to help the Nets win the 1976 ABA title. The gratitude of the Nets' owner later proved to be short-lived.

porters, and TV cameramen showed up, but Dr. J and his bride, Turquoise Brown, did not. Accompanied by two close friends, they switched to another hotel where a judge married them. They celebrated with champagne, pretzels, and potato chips—in privacy.

The Nets roared through the 1974 playoffs. They polished off the Virginia Squires in five games, then swept the Kentucky Colonels in the Eastern Division finals. Game 3 was the only close one. With the score tied at 87 in the final seconds, Dr. J jumped off the wrong foot and floated off-balance across the foul circle while throwing up a one-hander that caught only net at the buzzer. The Nets won the other games by 13, 19, and 13-point margins, as Dr. J averaged 29.8 points per game.

A nine-day layoff awaiting the outcome of the Western finals did not slow the Nets. In the opener against the Utah Stars, Erving scored 47 and Kenon 18 with 20 rebounds to beat Utah 89-85. They romped through Game 2, 118-94, and took their third in a row, 103-100 in overtime, after Brian Taylor's three-pointer had tied it in regulation. The Stars salvaged one win before the Nets nailed down New York's first ABA championship, 110-100.

In addition to his first championship ring, Dr. J won another scoring title and the Most Valuable Player Award. Speaking of the Doctor, Coach Loughery said, "There's never been anybody else like him."

5

THE NBA AT LAST

Good teams win championships; great teams repeat. The Nets won more games in 1974-75 than the year before, but they went into the playoffs lacking the intensity and cohesion they had earlier achieved. Their season ended in a first-round loss to the St. Louis Spirits.

The ABA was falling apart as rapidly as the Nets. Several teams were running out of money. The Nets were among the more solvent clubs, but the disappointing end to the season prompted management to trade Paultz, Kenon, and Gale to the San Antonio Spurs. Wendell Ladner died in a plane crash during the off-season.

Three things seemed obvious to Dr. J in the fall of 1975. This would be the ABA's last season; only the best teams had a chance to be merged into the NBA; he would have to be virtually a one-man team if he wanted to go out on top. And he was. In the 1976-76 season, Erving

Dr. J was voted the MVP of the 1977 NBA All-Star Game. He hit for 30 points, including these two over Rick Barry, as Doug Collins looked on.

led the league in scoring and finished among the top 10 in every offensive category.

The Nets faced their former teammates on the Spurs in the playoff semi-finals, a series that featured plenty of elbowing, leaning, pushing, and mouthing off. The fury culminated in Game 4 when a flurry of fists touched off a bench-clearing five-minute brawl.

Dr. J led the Nets to a 116-101 opening win with 31 points. But the Nets went flat after that, losing 105-79 and 111-103. Trailing 108-107 with 20 seconds to play in Game 4, Dr. J took a pass from Taylor and powered to the hoop for a game-winning dunk. Fouled on the play, he sank the free throw for his 35th point and a 110-108 victory.

The teams split the next two games, the Spurs taking Game 6, 106-105, despite Erving's 41. The finale turned out to be an easy, peaceful win for the Nets, 121-114.

The Nets went into Denver to begin the final showdown against the heavily-favored Nuggets, led by veteran Dan Issel, defensive star Bobby Jones, and the rookie Skywalker Thompson who had thrilled the hometown crowd by almost out-shining the Doctor in the half-time dunking contest at the All-Star Game. Thompson had just come off one of the best freshman seasons in history, averaging 26 points and 6.4 rebounds per game. "Skywalker came in to the playoffs like a young gunslinger after me," Dr. J observed.

"When we got to the finals against Denver, people figured we didn't have a chance," recalled Erving. "We hadn't won a game in Denver all season and they had the home-court advantage."

Erving scored 93 points in the first two games. The Nets won only one of these games, taking the opener in Denver 120-118, on Erving's 15-foot jumper at the buzzer. The performance put Dr. J on the cover of *Sports Illustrated*, but only the record Denver crowd of 19,034 got to see it; there was no national television of the series.

In the last two minutes of a close Game 3, the Doctor was everywhere, blocking shots and breaking up plays on defense, and scoring the Nets' last eight points with a clinic of jumpers, reverse layups, and two-handed slams for a 117-111 win. "I feel like I can do just about anything I want to do," the rejuvenated Doctor said.

The series returned to New York with the Nets holding a 3-2 lead. But Game 6 belonged to Skywalker, who was on the way to a 42-point effort. The Nuggets led 80-58 late in the third quarter. During a time out, Coach Loughery put Dr. J on Skywalker's case. "He's killing us. Go get him."

The Doctor stuck himself in Thompson's face the rest of the night, while the Nets, especially Super John Williamson, got hot from the floor. The more they narrowed the score, the louder the Nassau Coliseum crowd became. Erving was a one-man wrecking crew. In the fourth quarter alone, he registered nine rebounds and five steals.

When Williamson's jumper from the corner put them into the lead, the crowd's cry shook the building. As the buzzer ended the 112-106 win, the fans went berserk, crashing through police barricades around the court and tearing up everything in sight. A writer for *Sports Illustrated* described Dr. J's series as "the greatest individual performance by a basketball player at any level anywhere."

Further evidence of the imminent demise of the ABA came when the commissioner could not even present Erving and the Nets with a new trophy. As a reward for their championship, the Nets were handed the same trophy they had won in 1974.

All three of Erving's preseason predictions came true. The ABA officially folded after the 1976 playoffs, and the Nets were one of only four ABA teams that had the $3.2 million to buy a ticket into the NBA. (Denver, San Antonio, and the Indiana Pacers were the others.) The way was opened for Dr. J to be seen by national audiences in 21 NBA cities. The Nets franchise instantly became more valuable, and since he was the franchise, Erving believed that made him more valuable too. He was aware that one reason the NBA had deigned to allow the Nets into their exclusive club was their desire to have the world's most spectacular player for a drawing card.

Once the merger was official, Erving called the Nets' owner, Roy Boe, on his promise of a post-merger raise. But the Doctor soon learned that going in for a dunk against a seven-foot center was kid stuff compared to wringing more money out of the club owner. Boe appealed to Erving's team loyalty; the Doctor wondered aloud if an owner's loyalty to his players meant anything. Erving was called "selfish" by the press. Angry and frustrated, he found the print press harder to overcome than a full-court press. "I feel tarnished," he said.

The Doctor had expected to play out his career with the Nets and had bought a 17-room, $250,000 house on Long Island for his growing family. But now he soured on the Nets and their owner. The joy he had felt at the opportunity to go up against the best the NBA had to offer turned bitter.

Boe knew that a disgruntled Dr. J had less value to the Nets than the price he could get for the star. When the Philadelphia 76ers put $3 million on the table, Boe took it, and sold the Doctor down the New Jersey Turnpike. Erving signed a six-year contract with the Sixers for a reported $3.5 million.

When Coach Kevin Loughery of the Nets heard his star player had been traded, he bitterly commented, "Get me to a bar. I may have to become a drinkster."

On the other hand, members of the Sixers could hardly be happier. Caldwell Jones, on first being told the news, fell to his knees and cried for joy. Doug Collins couldn't fall asleep that night because he was laughing so hard. And George McGinnis expostulated, "Me and the Doctor together? Oh, my God!"

Philadelphia fans had a reputation for being the toughest in the country, whether they were "rooting" for the 76ers, baseball Phillies, football Eagles, or hockey Flyers. When an athlete or team failed to deliver, they could show no mercy.

The Sixers had been contenders but not champions in the NBA. A new owner, F. Eugene Dixon, now promised the fans a winner, and spent millions to make good on his word. In addition to Erving, he had acquired George McGinnis, co-MVP with Erving in the ABA in 1975, and ABA shot-blocking center Caldwell Jones. The team included potential all-pro guard Doug Collins; the unrestrained Lloyd B. Free, who was sometimes called "the Prince of Midair" but who later changed his name legally to World B. Free

Portland Trailblazer Bill Walton frustrated Dr. J and the Philadelphia 76ers in the 1977 NBA finals.

and believed that *he* was the most spectacular player in the world; Joe "Jellybean" Bryant, another expert at the playground game; and a 19-year-old rookie, 6'11" 265-pound Darryl Dawkins, alias Double D, alias Chocolate Thunder, alias Zandokan the Mad Dunker, who specialized in "teeth-shaking, glass-breaking, rump-roasting, bun-toasting, wham-bam, I-am jam."

Pat Williams, the Sixers' general manager, enthusiastically declared the team "the most exciting, breathtaking team in the history of sports in this country." Substitute forward Steve Mix saw his mates from another viewpoint. "Can you believe the head cases on this team?" he asked.

Philadelphia fans welcomed Dr. J with unrestrained enthusiasm, but the players greeted him with mixed feelings. McGinnis, who had played in Erving's shadow in the ABA, felt instantly eclipsed again. Others, acknowledging that Erving was a winner, fretted that his presence would mean less playing time or recognition for them.

Early in the season, Dr. J began to feel as if he was back in the Rucker League in Harlem. The 76ers carried the playground game to new levels. Fans flocked to see the Sixers' All-Star Flying Circus.

By the 1977 All-Star Game, Erving and the others who had come from the ABA felt they had proved they belonged in the NBA. Ten of the 24 players chosen for the game had played in the ABA. Dr. J buried the "minor league" rap for good, pouring in 30 points and taking home the All-Star MVP Award.

Yet all was not well with the "breathtaking team." Erving found that he was the only one going all out on every play on both offense and defense. "Hey, easy man," a teammate complained. "You're working too hard." Whenever he got hot, draining several shots in a row, the Doctor was shocked when his own teammates shut him down by not giving him the ball.

Few teammates were friends off the court and Coach Gene Shue did little to instill harmony. Lloyd Free summed up what was wrong when he called the crucial last minutes of a Sixers game "the time when we start hating each other."

Despite their failings as a team, the 76ers were so talented that they were too good to lose, and romped to the Atlantic Division title. They needed all seven games to get past the Boston Celtics and another six to beat the surprising Houston Rockets. They then found themselves in the playoff finals against the Portland Trailblazers, who were led by Bill Walton.

Recalling his one-man show that had brought the Nets the 1976 title, Dr. J set out to beat the 7'0" Walton. If it had to come to a game of one-on-one, he would take it to the big redhead, the best shot blocker in the NBA. Playing like the young Doctor of the playground, Erving demolished Walton in the first two games. Game 2 ended in a bench-clearing brawl touched off by the Blazers after Maurice Lucas and Lloyd Neal resorted to using their shoulders and elbows in an effort to stop the Doctor. Even coaches and fans got sucked into the fray. But the battle took all the fight out of the Sixers and pumped up the Blazers. They crushed the Sixers in the next three games.

Feeling like a man playing one-on-five, Dr. J tried to carry the Sixers on his own wings in Game 6 in Portland. He scored 40 points and kept his team close, but they came up short.

At the age of 28, Erving's knees felt the wear and tear of thousands of hard landings following high leaps. The infighting and personal enmities among the 76ers that drained the team's potential also sapped Erving's energy and enthusiasm, turning him into a passive player at times. Neither his flights to the hoop nor his stats were as high as in his ABA days. On the road he kept to himself, eating alone, watching TV in his room. He felt lonely and spent.

The 76ers made a quick exit from the 1978 playoffs, and that summer Erving attended a family reunion in South Carolina. Feeling sorry for himself following the dismal season, he was uplifted by meeting relatives he never knew existed and connecting with them.

"There were people I didn't even know who really cared about me," he discovered. "And I felt all that love passing through me. It was a very strange and wonderful feeling. My Uncle Alphonse said, 'Somebody along the line really laid a blessing on you.'"

Realizing there was no love lost among their collection of self-labeled all-stars, the management of the 76ers made some changes. They got rid of Free and McGinnis, and brought in the former ABA all-round star Bobby Jones. Rookie guard Maurice Cheeks helped the concept of teamwork as a master passer and stealer. Billy Cunningham became head coach; he wasted no time making it clear that there would be only one Main Man on the 76ers.

"Julius is one of the most level-headed players I have ever known," he said. "He understands himself and his teammates. I can think of no one I'd rather build a team around." Cunningham appointed Erving the captain of the team.

Once again the Doctor felt that he was out in front, but this time he would be leading a team, not carrying it. "It's going to be a lot more challenging," he said. "And I'm ready to accept the challenge."

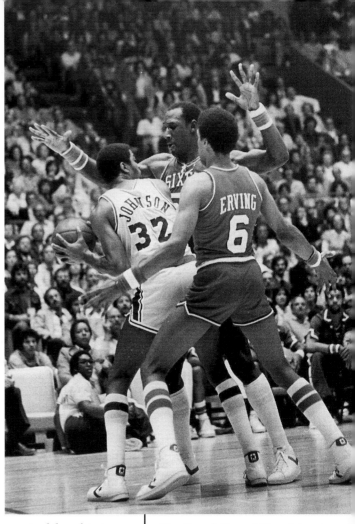

Dr. J and Darryl Dawkins try to trap Earvin "Magic" Johnson in the fifth game of the 1980 NBA finals. In the final game of the series, the rookie stepped in for an ailing Kareem Abdul-Jabbar and dealt a death blow to the 76ers' hopes.

It took a year for the new Sixers to blend into a winning combination, and when they did, they found two new obstacles in their path to the top: Larry Bird and Magic Johnson. In the fall of 1979, Bird made his debut with the Celtics, and Johnson joined the legendary Kareem Abdul-Jabbar in Los Angeles. For most of the next decade, the Lakers, Celtics, and 76ers would dominate the NBA.

If anything, the arrival of these rivals to the Doctor's title of King of the Court put new life into the 30-year-old Erving. "I haven't felt so good physically or mentally since my rookie year," he exclaimed, after finishing among the top 10 in scoring, steals, and blocked shots. What he had lost in spring or speed, he made up for in knowledge of the game. He still believed he could do anything on the court. It just took a little more thought and planning. Once in a while, a flash of the old razzle-dazzle blew the minds of fans and fellow pros.

After knocking off Larry Bird and the Celtics in the 1980 semifinals, the Sixers had to get by the Lakers to earn an NBA title ring. The teams split the first two games in Los Angeles. But home cooking did not lift the Sixers; they trailed for most of the night and lost Game 3 at the Spectrum 111-101. The frustrated and angry Philadelphia boo birds, sensing another late-season flop, got louder and ruder as the minutes ticked away.

The Sixers silenced the fans by running up a big lead early in Game 4, but the chorus reconvened as the lead dwindled down to four late in the fourth quarter. Dr. J got the ball, and suddenly he was bearing down on the 7'2" Kareem. With the giant defender waving his arms, Erving lifted off. Soaring toward the hoop, he pumped once to the right side, then, seemingly suspended in midair, snatched the ball away from Kareem's clawing reach and lightly kissed it off the glass to the left of the rim before descending. "I didn't plan that" he said after the game. "A force beyond me allowed that to happen."

Despite a leg injury that left Kareem limping at the end of Game 5, the Lakers had enough firepower to overcome Dr J's 36 points and win, 108-103. The Sixers were encouraged when they heard that Kareem would not suit up for Game 6, but they were unaware that a new star was ready to shine with the kind of amazing performance the Doctor had once patented. The finale belonged to Magic Johnson. The 6′9″ guard played every position and posted 42 points, 15 rebounds, 7 assists, and 3 steals. At age 20, Johnson wore the NBA world championship ring.

Dr. J had seen the future.

6

DARING TO BE GREAT

In 1981, the competition for the Most Valuable Player award was intense. Strong candidates included Kareem Abdul-Jabbar, Magic Johnson, Larry Bird, plus newcomers Isiah Thomas, James Worthy, Charles Barkley, and Michael Jordan. But at age 31, Dr. J walked off with the award, the first noncenter in 17 years to win the NBA's top honor.

Unfortunately, another pattern remained unbroken. After taking a 3-1 lead over the Celtics in the playoff semifinals, the Sixers lost the next three. A year after having been torched by Magic Johnson, Larry Bird repeated the trick, single-handedly nullifying Erving's heroic efforts in the last five minutes of the final game.

The 1982 playoffs looked a lot like the 1981 playoffs. For the third year in a row, the Sixers took a 3-1 lead over the Celtics in the Eastern Division finals. Again the Celtics fought back to

Revenge is sweet. In 1983, Dr. J and the 76ers won the NBA championship by beating a Los Angeles Lakers team led by Magic Johnson.

force a deciding Game 7, this time in Boston, where they were all but unbeatable.

Desperate to loosen the tightness that had wrapped itself around the Sixers, coach Cunningham ordered the loose-lipped Darryl Dawkins to lighten them up with jokes and wisecracks just before game time. It worked. Dr. J poured in 29 as part of a total team effort and the Sixers romped, 120-106.

But the win just enabled them to step in front of the juggernaut from the West Coast, the Lakers, who had won eight straight to reach the finals. Abdul-Jabbar, Johnson, Worthy, and company were too much for anyone to stop. They subdued the Sixers in six.

In the last game, Erving carried his team with an eight-point outburst in two minutes that brought the Sixers even. Then something happened that would have never occurred five years earlier. Charging the rim for a high-flying dunk that would have put the 76ers in the lead, Dr J felt his shot blocked from behind.

After five years of near misses, Erving, now 32, had no thought of quitting the chase for an elusive NBA title. "Unless you dare to put yourself at center stage, dare to be great, you never can be," he said in a postgame interview. "I'm going to keep daring. As I dared in the past, I'll dare in the future."

The playoff losses had exposed the Sixers' main weakness compared to the Lakers and Celtics. When Larry Bird was tied up, he had Kevin McHale and Dennis Johnson to go to. When Kareem was stopped, he had Magic Johnson or James Worthy to help out. Dr. J had no such help. The Sixers remedied that during the off-season by signing free agent Moses Malone, the 1981-82 MVP who had averaged 31.1 points and 14.7 rebounds.

Moses was as unlike Dr. J as he could be: small hands, low leaping and flying ability, no speed. He did not float or fake or slice his opponents; he pounded away at them relentlessly in the paint and under the hoop. But Erving and Malone had one thing in common. "He works so hard," someone said of Malone, "that he makes the other players feel guilty if they don't put out as much effort."

The ease with which Erving seemed to make his moves on the court belied the hours of practice, of trial and error, trying to improve the old and improvise the new. "Even now I'll be watching a game somewhere and I'll see somebody do something that'll remind me of something I've forgotten—some little move maybe. I'll practice it a little, and I've got it back, and when the right situation comes along, maybe I've got a little edge I didn't have before."

In his 11th year as a pro, Dr. J had some adjustments to make. For the first time, he was not the top gun. "When you become the second or third option on a play," he said, "it requires some adjustments. Sometimes I wasn't able to make that adjustment. I'd get lost, out of my rhythm. That's when you have to step back and regroup."

But the old pro adjusted, and the Sixers became a team that worked so smoothly and consistently they were on the way to setting the NBA record for regular-season wins before they eased up at the end and rested for the playoffs. They polished off two postseason challengers in nine games, and, like the predictable shootout in the last reel of a western movie, squared off against the Lakers in the showdown.

Freed of the burden of carrying the team alone, a renewed Dr. J played his consummate game; he dunked and rebounded, fed Malone, and blocked shots. With Malone dominating the boards, the Lakers never knew what hit them as the Sixers wiped them out in four straight.

"That was for Doc," Malone said amid the victory celebration in the locker room. "I wanted to be able to say that I played on a world championship team with Dr. J."

Julius Erving finally had an NBA ring to go with his ABA jewelry. It was his last. With each passing year he lost a step, and the younger acrobats fresh off the playgrounds took up more of the spotlight.

By 1986, Erving felt it was time to devote more time to his numerous charities, pursue other accomplishments in other fields, and spend more time with his four children, Cheo, Julius III, Jazmin, and Cory. He became a partner in a group that bought the Philadelphia Coca-Cola Bottling Company, the fourth largest black-owned business in the country at that time. He branched out into other businesses, and, behind the wheel of his Maserati, began to look more like the successful businessman he was becoming. In addition, he devoted himself to numerous charitable causes, including the Hemophilia Foundation, the Lupus Foundation, the March of Dimes, and the Special Olympics.

In the spring of 1986, Erving made good on a promise he had made to his mother 15 years

A sad Julius Erving held the ball aloft in a final salute to the fans as he walked off the court in his last game.

earlier. He returned to UMass and earned a degree in business.

Dr. J announced that he would retire at the end of the 1986-87 season. His final tour around the league gave fans and players a chance to give him deep and sincere ovations of thanks and appreciation.

"The Doc changed basketball," Magic Johnson said. "The Doc went past jumps, hooks, sets, went past everything, and made the playground official."

"I've never heard anybody knock him or express jealousy, said star forward Dominique Wilkins. "I can't name you one other player who has that status."

As always, Erving kept his cool amid the shower of gifts and accolades—except in his final game against the Nets. At halftime, his old red, white, and blue Nets uniform, with the number 32 on it, hung high in the air above the court. "I can't bear to look up there," Erving told the crowd, which included his mother, his UMass coach Jack Leaman, and many of his former Nets teammates. Then he looked up, and tears flowed down his face for the first time since his brother died.

Dr. J dipped into the fountain of youth one more time as the season ended, scoring 38 points in a display that featured every kind of scoring in the books, from three-pointers to no-doubt-about-it dunks. He became the third player, after Wilt Chamberlain and Abdul-Jabbar, to score 30,000 points in a career.

When Julius Erving was inducted into the Basketball Hall of Fame in 1992, reporters asked the usual questions of players and coaches, including, "How did Dr. J compare to Michael Jordan?" Billy Cunningham responded, "Julius was the best player I've ever seen in the open court, and that includes Jordan." Hubie Brown, who coached against both players, said Erving "made plays no one has seen before or since, plays that not even Michael Jordan could do."

Onetime ABA star Steve Jones rated them equally "as players who have no limits." But he added that "Julius played much higher above the rim."

Erving was not concerned with ratings and comparisons. He had been given a gift, but he also knew that gift would have meant nothing without countless hours of hard work to make something of it. "I want young people to see I am a hard-working successful black man," he said. Lest they think it would be easy to take the playground game and turn it into a career, he told kids, "There are 250 pro basketball players in a country of 250 million people. You think you're one in a million? If there were a million guys lined up here, could you beat them all one-on-one?"

Detroit Pistons' star Isiah Thomas summed it up when he said, "You have been an inspiration, a leader, and a perfect role model for me and all the other NBA players. You have made the path much smoother for us younger guys to follow."

To follow, one might add, but not to duplicate. There would never be another Dr. J.

The Doctor wore a cap and gown as he received his bachelor's degree in business from the University of Massachusetts in 1986.

STATISTICS

JULIUS WINFIELD ERVING II

SEASON	TEAM	G	MIN	FGM	FGA	PCT	FTM	FTA	PCT	RBD	AST	PTS	AVG
1971-72	VA	84	3513	910	1826	.493	467	627	.745	1319	335	2290	27.3
1972-73	VA	71	2993	894	1804	.496	475	612	.776	867	298	2268	**31.9**
1973-74	NY	84	3398	914	1785	.512	454	583	.766	899	434	2299	**27.4**
1974-75	NY	84	3402	914	1806	.506	486	606	.799	914	462	2343	27.9
1975-76	NY	84	3244	949	1873	.507	530	662	.801	925	423	2462	**29.3**
1976-77	Phil	82	2940	685	1373	.499	400	515	.777	695	306	1770	21.6
1977-78	Phil	74	2429	611	1217	.502	306	362	.845	481	279	1528	20.6
1978-79	Phil	78	2802	715	1455	.491	373	501	.745	564	357	1803	23.1
1979-80	Phil	78	2812	838	1614	.519	420	534	.787	576	355	2100	26.9
1980-81	Phil	82	2874	794	1524	.521	422	536	.787	657	364	2014	24.6
1981-82	Phil	81	2789	780	1428	.546	411	539	.763	557	319	1974	24.4
1982-83	Phil	72	2421	605	1170	.517	330	435	.759	491	263	1542	21.4
1983-84	Phil	77	2883	678	1324	.512	364	483	.754	532	309	1727	22.4
1984-85	Phil	78	2535	610	1236	.494	338	442	.765	414	233	1561	20.0
1985-86	Phil	74	2474	521	1085	.480	289	368	.785	370	248	1340	18.1
1986-87	Phil	60	1918	400	850	.471	191	235	.813	264	191	1005	16.8
Reg. Season Totals		1243	45227	11818	23370	.507	6256	8052	.777	10725	5176	30026	24.2
Playoff Totals		189	7352	1769	3563	.496	1015	1308	.776	1611	941	4580	24.2
All-Star Totals		16	550	123	249	.494	73	91	.802	106	59	321	20.0

G	games
MIN	minutes
FGA	field goals attempted
FGM	field goals made
PCT	percent
FTA	free throws attempted
FTM	free throws made
RBD	rebounds
AST	assists
PTS	points
AVG	scoring average

bold indicates league-leading figures

JULIUS ERVING
A CHRONOLOGY

1950   Born in Hempstead, New York

1968   Enrolls at University of Massachusetts

1971   Signs with Virginia Squires of the ABA

1972   Named to ABA All-Rookie Team

1973   Leads the ABA in scoring; named to First-Team ABA; sold to the New York Nets

1974   Marries Turquoise Brown; named Most Valuable Player, ABA season and playoffs; wins second scoring title

1975   Scores career high of 63 points against the San Diego Conquistadors on February 14; named ABA co-MVP

1976   Named Most Valuable Player ABA season and playoffs; wins third scoring title; wins ABA championship with Nets; sold to Philadelphia 76ers; ends ABA career averaging 28.7 points and 12.1 rebounds per game

1977   Named NBA All-Star Game MVP

1981   Named NBA MVP

1983   Named NBA All-Star Game MVP; wins NBA championship with 76ers

1986   Receives a bachelor's degree in business from the University of Massachusetts

1987   Scores 30,000th point; retires from pro basketball

1992   Inducted into Basketball Hall of Fame

SUGGESTIONS FOR FURTHER READING

Axthelm, Pete. *The City Game: Basketball from the Garden to the Playground.* New York: Penguin, 1982.

Bell, Marty. *The Legend of Dr. J.* New York: Signet, 1976.

Pluto, Terry. *Loose Balls: The Short, Wild Life of the American Basketball Association as Told by the Players, Coaches, and Movers and Shakers Who Made It Happen.* New York: Simon & Schuster, 1990.

Sabin, Lou. *Hot Shots of Pro Basketball.* New York: Random House, 1974.

Thomas, D. *Dr. J.* Los Angeles: Holoway House, 1980.

INDEX

ABOUT THE AUTHOR

Norman Macht was a general manager for two minor league baseball organizations. He has written for *The Sporting News* and *Baseball Digest,* and is the author of more than a half dozen books in Chelsea House's BASEBALL LEGENDS series.